# All About Y...

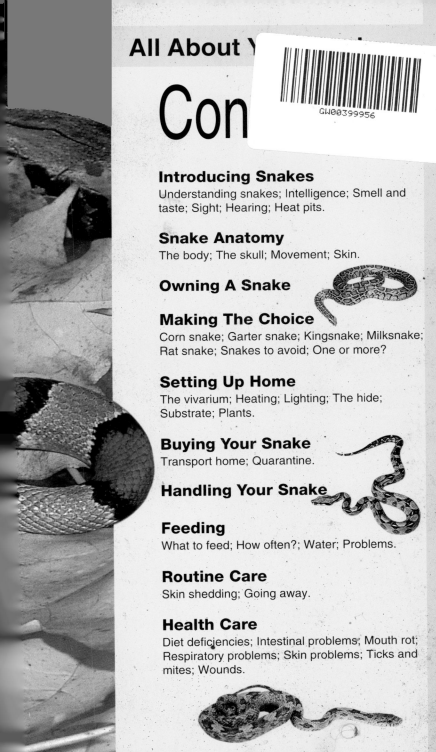

# Con...

*Californian Kingsnake: snakes are beautiful to look at and fascinating to watch.*

S nakes are reptiles that have been on the earth for millions of years, and have adapted to survive in many habitats in nearly all the world's regions, except the very coldest. Snakes live in deserts, rain forests, savannahs, marshlands, seas and rivers. As well as the terrestrial (ground) snakes, many snakes, such as the boa constrictor, are arboreal (tree-dwelling), others – the mole viper for example, live in burrows.

Snakes vary tremendously in appearance, ranging from the smallest worm snake at less than six inches (15.25 cm), to the very largest – the green anaconda and reticulated python – which grow more than 30 feet (nine metres). They come in all colours, and in a wide range of patterns which act as camouflage or as a warning to would-be predators.

Snake-keeping is becoming increasingly popular, and some snakes make excellent pets.

- They are clean.
- They produce little mess.
- Being without hair or feathers, they do not produce allergic reactions in sensitive people.
- Caring for a snake is relatively straightforward, and not too time-consuming.

Snakes are very beautiful, and fascinating to watch. A properly set-up vivarium (reptile house) could be a focal point in your home.

## Understanding Snakes

Snakes evolved from lizards. Over the years, they lost their limbs (along with their eyelids and external ears). In the most primitive snakes, such as pythons and boas, the remains of these limbs remain as a tiny pair of spurs at the base of the tail, and are often more highly-developed in males. In more advanced species, males often have a longer tail that tapers at the end, and females usually have a shorter, more stubby tail. Snakes can be probed to check their sex for certain, but this should only be done by experienced snake keepers.

Like all reptiles, snakes are cold-blooded, meaning they get their heat from the environment, rather than generating it internally, as mammals do. This makes snakes very energy-efficient, as their food intake needs to be substantially less than a similar sized warm-blooded animal that needs to use precious energy keeping its body warm.

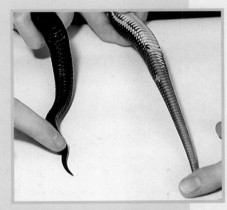

**Male black Kingsnake (left) and female Californian Kingsnake.**

*The flicking tongue is a means of 'tasting' smells.*

## Intelligence

Snakes are not as intelligent as birds or mammals, as they lack the large cerebral hemispheres of the brain that are responsible for learning. However, captive snakes soon learn routines, especially when it comes to their feeding times.

## Smell And Taste

Snakes can 'taste' smells. The flickering tongue, which some people wrongly believe is a stinging device, picks up small particles from the air. The tongue is then placed against a structure in the roof of the mouth called a 'Jacobson's organ', which consists of two cavities lined with a sensitive membrane able to identify the different smells or chemical 'cues'.

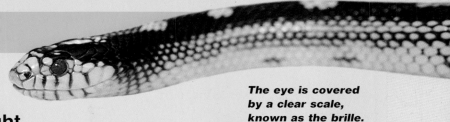

## Sight

In snakes, a clear, protective scale ('brille', or 'tertiary spectacle') covers the eye, instead of an eyelid. Different types of snakes have varying degrees of vision, and it is not certain whether snakes can perceive stationary objects. Tree snakes, (e.g. emerald tree boa) have acute vision. Often feeding on birds, they need to be fast and accurate when striking. Ground snakes (e.g. royal python) have fairly good sight, and are believed to have black-and-white vision. Burrowing snakes (e.g. burrowing viper) have no need for good eyesight, and so have developed less acute vision.

## Hearing

Snakes have no internal ear openings. They pick up vibrations from the ground with their body, but rely mainly on their other senses, which are far more acute.

## Heat Pits

Snakes that feed on warm-blooded prey have 'heat pits'. These are hollows with very sensitive membranes which can detect tiny changes in temperature, and so alert them to the presence and location of prey. Where the heat pits are situated varies. Boas and pythons have

*The heat pits on this Golden Python are located on the upper lip.*

them along their upper lip, and pit vipers have them as two openings, rather like nostrils, at the front of the face.

5

## The Body

Generally, vipers have about 100 ribs and the larger pythons have more than 400 (although, in each case, it depends on the taxon of snake). Each vertebrae (the individual bones of the spinal column) is attached to a pair of ribs. Many species of snake (e.g. cobra) can flatten their ribs in the neck when threatened to make themselves appear larger. The wider surface area also enables the snake to get more sun, a vital energy source.

Muscles ensure the snake's flexibility. There are muscles between the vertebrae and the ribs, in between the ribs, between the ribs and the skin, and even the skin has its own muscles.

*The musculature of a snake allows for tremendous flexibility.*

## The Skull

The snake's skull is supported by the first vertebra. The shape of the skull varies depending on the species and its needs. A burrowing snake needs a flat, thick head, whereas a tree snake needs a lighter, less cumbersome head. Many burrowing snakes actually have a head that is shaped like a shovel.

*The shape of the skull varies between species according to particular needs.*

Snakes have six rows of teeth that curve backwards to bring food down the throat, and to prevent live prey from escaping. The teeth break and are replaced frequently, ensuring the teeth are always sharp. Venomous snakes have maxillary teeth – or 'fangs' – which are replaced several times a year.

Venom flows down a hollow channel in the fangs when the snake bites its prey. Venom is precious to the snake, and is only used when there is a real threat – hence many bites are 'dry bites', where no venom is used.

## Movement

Snakes have evolved unique methods of movement. They press their body against the ground to grip it, while elongating their body lengthways. If put on a very smooth surface, such as a mirror, the snake would not be able to move forward, as the belly scales would not have an anchor to grip.

• Rectilinear – larger snakes, like the Burmese python, move by using their muscles to walk on their ribs. They drag themselves forward on their ribs, and so

# Snake Anatomy

*All snakes use a form of rectilinear movement.*

can move in a straight line. All snakes use a form of rectilinear movement in one degree or another (apart from some aquatic snakes).

• Serpentine – this is where the snake (e.g. cornsnake) propels itself forward in an S-bend and is the most common form of movement in snakes.

• Concertina – snakes such as the Burmese python, for example, move by scrunching up and then extending themselves forward.

• Sidewinding – this was developed to cope with the desert environment, which is difficult for snakes to otherwise manoeuvre in. Sidewinding snakes, (e.g. desert sidewinder), move by throwing themselves forward at a 45 degree angle, and the rest of the body follows on.

## Skin

The skin has adapted to the snake's way of life, and its temperature is entirely dependent on the surrounding environment. Snakes (e.g. banded rock rattler) that live in the desert need to have thick, rough scales to aid movement in the sand, whereas corn snakes are smooth because they can lever themselves through damp fields, bushes or forests in their natural American habitat.

Snakes shed to remove any parasites or damage to their skin. Young animals shed more frequently than older animals, sloughing off the old skin several times a year as they elongate and outgrow their epidermis. A snake suffering from a skin disease is also likely to shed more frequently.

*Snakes shed their skin to remove parasites and damaged areas.*

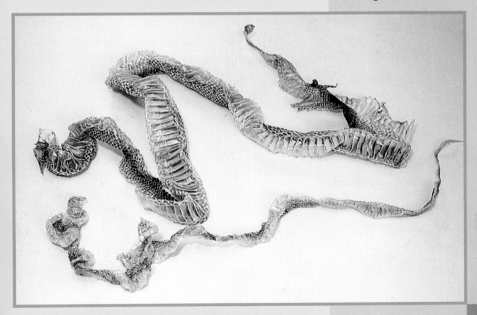

9

# Owning A Snake

**B**efore buying a snake, you should seriously consider whether you are able to look after it properly, but if you are unhappy handling dead animals, then perhaps you should reconsider your choice of pet.

• **Do you have the time and commitment to devote to snake-keeping?** It takes just 10 minutes a day to look after your snake – cleaning the water bowl and vivarium glass, removing faeces, and checking your snake is healthy. However, this needs to be done every day, in addition to a thorough weekly vivarium clean.

• **Can you afford to keep a snake?** The cost of buying your snake and setting it up in a comfortable home is not cheap. Maintaining it for the next 20 years or so is even costlier. Veterinary bills and feeding costs should also be considered, as should the slightly increased electricity bill from the vivarium heating/lighting.

• All snakes require whole, animal prey, be it rats, mice, fish or earthworms etc. The increased popularity of snake-keeping means many pet stores sell frozen prey – but if you are at all squeamish, perhaps you consider a different choice of pet.

*Taking on a snake needs very careful consideration.*

# Making The Choice

**B**efore buying a snake, you should give careful consideration to what is going to be right for you. The principle consideration should be size – not of the snake when you purchase it, but the size to which it will eventually grow.

It is all too easy to go for a very cute Burmese python only to discover, too late, that it will grow very large indeed. The challenges involved in caging a 15 ft (4.57 metres) python need to be taken into consideration when you buy the hatchling. In recent years, zoos and pet shops have been left to cope with these impulse buys when they get too large for their owners to manage, and many now refuse to accept them.

Nowadays, many snakes are bred in captivity, and this is the best choice if you are starting out. The novice snake-keeper should choose a snake that is easy to manage, straightforward to feed, and will thrive in a basic vivarium set-up. There are many species of snake (mostly ground-dwellers) which meet all the criteria for an ideal pet snake.

## Corn Snake

Arguably the best snake for the novice keeper, the North American corn snake, *Elaphe guttatta*, is common on farms, as well as in damper habitats. It is captive bred in large numbers, and is now produced in a wide range of patterns and colours.
• Average size of 3-4 feet (0.91-1.22 metres), some grow larger.
• Easy to feed.
• Thrives in captivity.
• Cheap and readily available.

*The corn snake is available in a wide range of colours and patterns.*

# Making The Choice

## Garter Snake

From north and central America, the garter snake (members of the genus *Themnophis*) often lives near water in the wild, so it needs a higher humidity and, like all snakes, access to water. It should also have dry substrate (ground covering) or skin rot can occur. Garter Snakes will feed on fish, although an exclusively fish diet will result in a thiamine deficiency.

*The garter snake needs high humidity.*

- Small (around 2-3 ft/0.61-0.91 metres), and very attractive.
- Garter snakes breed readily in captivity.
- Very affordable price.
- Easy availability.

## Kingsnake

Kingsnakes are so-named because of their habit of preying on other snakes but they are, nonetheless, excellent as pets. In captivity, they usually feed on relatively small rodents and, as their hatchlings are slightly larger than those of corn or garter snakes, the babies often start feeding straightaway on baby mice.

The scientific name of the common kingsnake (*Lampropeltis getula*) is derived from the latin for 'shiny shields', as the scales are very smooth and glossy. The bold black and yellow coloration is very striking, but captive breeding has also produced albinos and many other colours and patterns.

*Californian Kingsnake showing the classic yellow and black colouring.*

There are a number of species and many sub-species. Generally, they live in hot, desert-type environments, so need an overhead heat source (safely protected to avoid contact burns), and a temperature of around 82 degrees Fahrenheit (28 degrees Centigrade).
• Easy to handle and rarely bite.
• Should be kept individually, especially when being fed, to avoid cannibalism.
• More expensive than garter or corn snake, but still an affordable choice.
• Some individuals can grow up to 6 $^1/_2$ feet (2 metres) in length, though it is rare for them to reach this length.

## Milksnake

Another member of the *Lampropeltis* genus is the milksnake (*Lampropeltis triangulum*). There are many sub-species, but all share the incredible red, black and yellow coloration which mimics the venomous coral snakes. Milksnakes were so-named because they are often found living in or near cattle sheds in America. It was widely believed that they drank milk from the udders of cows, but it is now known that they inhabit such places due to the high rodent population, which offers abundant food.
• Thrives in captivity.
• Hatchling milksnakes are so small that feeding them may prove too great a challenge for the amateur.
• More expensive than the other varieties recommended.
• Average size of 3-4 feet (0.91-1.22 metres), some grow larger.

*Sinaloan Milksnake: All sub-species share the dramatic red, black and yellow coloration.*

## Rat Snake

The rat snake (*Elaphe* genus) is very widespread, but the best captives are those from North America. Asian and European rat snakes can be delicate and difficult to care for (even if captive-bred) and are best left to experienced keepers. The most suitable rat snake for beginners is the grey rat (*Elaphe obsoleta*) as the others, such as the black rat and the yellow rat, can be quite aggressive. The grey rat snake may not have the obvious beauty of the milksnakes, but has much in its favour:

- Placid nature.
- Easy to care for.
- Breeds well in captivity.
- Moderate size, reaching about 4 ft in length (1.22 metres).
- Very affordable.

*Texas Rat Snake: these snakes have a placid approach to life.*

## Snakes To Avoid

Large boas and pythons should be avoided, even babies, as the long-term commitment should be considered. Anacondas and reticulated pythons in particular should not be considered

*Beautiful to look at, but this Burmese Python measures 16ft in length.*

under any circumstances. Anacondas grow to around 20-22 feet (6-6.5 metres) and pythons grow in excess of 30 feet (9.15 metres); both can be aggressive. Venomous snakes should obviously not be contemplated.

## One Or More?

It is generally better to keep snakes singly, although female corn snakes, rat snakes, and garter snakes can be kept together. Males can live happily together, but territorial problems can sometimes occur, especially in the breeding season if a female is present. Kingsnakes of either sex are cannibalistic, and should always be kept singly. Milksnakes are from the same family as the king snake, so caution should be exercised if they are kept in groups.

That some snakes can 'fly'? Snakes of the genus Chrysopelia can spread their ribs to form a large fold of skin which they use to glide from tree to tree.

*Rat Snakes will live peaceably together, but it is preferable to keep to a single sex.*

**I**n the wild, snakes will spend most of their time hiding. In captivity, they can be happy in quite a bare vivarium, as long as their biological needs are seen to, and they feel safe. A hide (see Decor) is therefore essential.

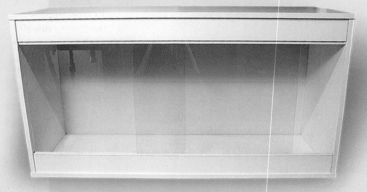

*The accommodation must grow with your snake.*

## The Vivarium

Newly-hatched snakes can be kept in a small container where they will feel secure and be easy to maintain. Your pet store should stock suitable pet carriers or fauna boxes, or you could use any suitable plastic container with a securely fitting lid. If you choose this option, remember to drill some holes in the side for ventilation.

As your snake grows, so should its housing. As a general rule, the length of the enclosure should be at least a third of the length of the snake. The shape of the vivarium will also depend on the type of snake. A ground snake will need as much floor space as possible, whereas a tree-dwelling snake will need a taller vivarium. Ideally, the vivarium colour should be dark to reduce stress levels in the snake.

The most important consideration is to make the vivarium completely escape-proof. Snakes are nature's master escapees, and, if there is a loophole in your tank security, your snake will exploit it!

For larger snakes, there is a wide range of ready-made vivaria available. An all-glass aquarium, fitted with a secure vivarium lid, is a popular option. These are also suitable for burrowing snakes which need a good depth of substrate, or for semi-aquatic species, such as garter snakes. Glass tanks can have security problems, so be sure the lid is absolutely safe.

Another popular option is the melamine vivarium. This normally comes in the form of a wooden box with sliding glass doors at the front. You may find a ready-to-go vivarium, complete with lights, heating etc., but these are generally an expensive option.

## Heating

Being cold-blooded, snakes rely on heat for their energy and well-being. The **heat mat** is the most common form of heating for snakes. It is placed *under* a glass tank. Some owners put it along the back wall, on the outside of the tank. Be warned that heat mats may sometimes crack the glass. The heat mat

DID YOU KNOW?

That snakes have to shed their skin in order to grow? When they are young snakes may shed their skin as much as six or seven times a year but when adult they may only shed once a year.

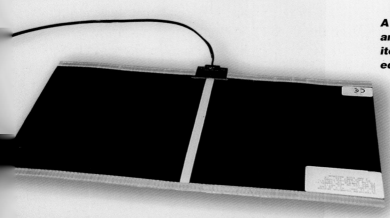

*A heat mat is an essential item of equipment.*

should be approximately one-third to one-half of the floor area of the vivarium. It should never exceed one-half of the floor area, as the snake needs to be able to escape from the heat into a cooler area. It is always safer to use a thermostat with any heating device – including a heat mat – so that a maximum temperature can be set.

As a rough guide, most snakes in captivity require a daytime temperature of around 80 degrees

*A basking lamp must be positioned carefully.*

Fahrenheit (28 C). Night temperatures should be several degrees lower (around 75 F/24 C). A hot spot, for basking, of about 90 F/32.5 C should also be provided.

## Lighting

Snakes do not require special lighting, but a low level ultraviolet light (UVB 2 per cent) can be beneficial to them. A number of fluorescent light tubes are available for reptiles, and your retailer will be able to advise you on a suitable model. Alternatively, many snake keepers use a normal household light-bulb. Care should be taken with this option, as these emit heat as well as light (see Heating, above), and they do not emit the appropriate UV wavelength.

Lighting should not be left on for 24 hours. It is important to consider the snake's life in the wild, and how it would respond to light and dark over the course of 24 hours (known as the photoperiod). For example, a tropical snake, such as the boa constrictor, will need 12 hours of light and 12 hours of dark.

*Fluoresce light tube are availa for reptile*

## The Hide

A hide is very important to snakes. In the wild, snakes can be attacked and killed by a number of

*Hides are generally made from cork bark.*

birds and animals, and spend much of their time in a safe retreat, such as a crevice or burrow. Without a hide, a snake may feel vulnerable and refuse to eat.

The hide you provide should be small, dark, and enclosed on all sides, with an access hole or entrance. When the snake is in the hide, it should be able to touch at least three sides Cork bark is generally used as a hide, but a number of purpose-built models are now available. It is worth having a hide in the warm part of the vivarium, as well as in the cool, so the snake can decide what suits it best.

## Substrate

Substrate can be gravel, bark chippings or newspaper. Newspaper may not look very pretty, but it is clean, safe, and cheap. Substrates such as bark chippings or gravel look attractive, but are both readily ingested and often induce gastrointestinal obstructions. Wood shavings can irritate the lungs and the oils can be toxic to snakes.

## Plants

Artificial plants will make your vivarium more attractive and will give your snake opportunities for climbing. Arboreal (tree-dwelling) species will also need sturdy branches to climb.

# Buying Your Snake

**M**any reputable pet stores, and reptile specialists stock snakes, and knowledgeable staff will be available to help you make your choice. Before buying a snake, inspect the conditions in which it has been kept. The cage should be clean, a reasonable size, not overcrowded, and the snake should have access to water and heat.

Now turn your attention to the snake.

Does the snake
• Have bright eyes?
• Look the correct weight, with no backbone visible?
• Have a clean nose, mouth and eyes, free of discharge?
• Have a smooth outline – free of lumps and bumps?
• Have all its scales? (If scales are missing, the wound should be well-healed.)
• Have tiny dots between the scales? Mites are very contagious. If the snake has mites, other snakes in the same establishment can also have them, so it is worth going elsewhere.
• Have breathing difficulties? If so, serious health problems could be responsible.

The snake should be alert, and easy to handle. A snake of about six months is ideal for a beginner. By then, you will know that it is feeding well, and it will be more used to being handled.

*Eastern Common Garter Snake: a top-class specimen.*

## Transport Home

A pillowcase, knotted at the top, is ideal for transporting the snake home, taking it to the vet, or for when you are cleaning out the vivarium. The pillowcase can be put in a bare plastic tank for extra security.

## Quarantine

Never introduce newly-acquired specimens into an enclosure inhabited by established snakes. If your snake is ill, symptoms may not become apparent for a number of weeks, so it is advisable to use a quarantine tank for up to two months, so you can ensure the new arrival is healthy and feeding adequately.

# Handling Your Snake

I f you choose one of the species highlighted earlier in this book, handling your snake should not present any problems. If your animal is aggressive or nervous at first, it is probably because it is threatened – frequent handling will make it worse. Leave it for about seven days, and then open its tank and let it come to you. Once out of its housing, it can be handled. It should become more accustomed to your scent, and will stop feeling threatened. A bite from a non-venomous snake is like a series of very small pinpricks, but it can be painful. If you handle your snake properly, this should be a very rare occurrence.

*Once your snake has had a chance to settle, handling rarely causes a problem.*

• In the wild, most threats to a snake come from above. In captivity, the snake learns that food comes from above. Stroking the snake gently with a snake hook will dissipate the food response before you put your hands in the vivarium to remove the snake.

*When your snake is bigger, make sure the body is fully supported.*

• You should only hold the snake's head if it is known to be aggressive; in tame, docile snakes it is preferable to hold them three to four inches (7.5-10 cm) below the head. Although this gives it the opportunity to bite you, this handling method is much kinder. Holding the head of a tame snake may encourage it to be aggressive.

• It is *very* important to support the body of the snake, but it will generally find its most comfortable position, winding around our hand or arm just as it would a branch.

• Hold your snake firmly but not roughly. Gripping it too hard could injure it.

• Act calmly and confidently. Do not make sudden movements which could alarm your snake.

• Never place a snake around your neck.

Like many animals, snakes can carry *Salmonella*, so you should always wash your hands after handling. Snakes measuring 8 ft (2.43 metres) or more should be supported by no less than two people.

# Feeding

*This Californian Kingsnake will need feeding every 14 days.*

## What To Feed

All snakes are totally carnivorous and eat by swallowing whole prey items. To enable the snake to breathe while swallowing its prey whole, it extends its epiglottis (extension of the windpipe) from the base of its mouth to underneath the prey to reach air at the front of the mouth.

The vast diversity of snake species means that there is a huge range of natural prey, from worms, insects, lizards, frogs, fish and mammals, to other snakes. In the UK, all vertebrate snake food must be dead. In captivity, however, we tend to feed snakes on rodents bred for this purpose. Most baby snakes will thrive on a diet of day-old mice or rats, called pinkies. As the snake grows, it tackles bigger prey and a large python will cope with rabbits. Most of the moderate-sized captive snakes are fed adult mice; the larger snakes are fed on rats.

## How Often?

Your snake should only be fed once it has digested its previous meal, which will be obvious after defecation. As a rule, an adult corn snake or kingsnake would need to be fed every 14 days, although each individual is different. Overfed snakes become obese and this is both unsightly and dangerous for the health of the animal. If breeding, increase the food intake prior to mating as a female will not eat while she is gravid (pregnant or carrying eggs). Juvenile snakes will need to be fed more often – about every four days should suffice.

# Water

Water is vital to a snake's well-being, so you should ensure that your snake's water bowl is always clean and filled with fresh water. The water is not only for drinking, it is also important for creating sufficient humidity in the vivarium. Many snakes will want to bathe occasionally, so the bowl should be large enough to do this. Many captive snakes defecate while bathing, so be sure to change the water regularly. Use a heavy bowl that the snake cannot overturn.

# Problems

Occasionally, snakes stop feeding. This can be for a variety of reasons. The two most common times are during skin shedding and pregnancy, or, in the case of pythons, when they are incubating eggs. Newly-acquired snakes sometimes refuse food until they have settled into their new environment, and for this reason, it is advisable not to offer food during the first week, as it could cause stress to the snake.

In the wild, fasting for extended periods – during drought or other adverse weather conditions – is a natural experience. In captivity, snakes occasionally fast and this is not normally a problem – they resume eating when they are hungry.

*Fresh water must be readily available.*

If your snake refuses to eat, and loses weight or otherwise deteriorates, consult your veterinary surgeon. If juveniles refuse food, seek help sooner rather than later, as the younger the snake, the less time it can go without food.

*The vivarium will need a thorough clean once a month.*

Cleaning the vivarium should be carried out on an as-needed basis. Remove any waste material, sloughed skin or other debris as soon as it is sighted. Ensure the water bowl is clean and that the water is fresh at all times. Many snakes defecate in their water bowl, so pay particular attention to this.

About once a month, you should strip down the cage and thoroughly clean with a disinfectant designed for the purpose. Keep one object – such as a stone – that is not cleaned. It will retain the snake's scent and so will help to reduce the snake's stress levels when faced with a new-smelling clean environment. A whole range of cleaning products for reptile habitats are now available from good pet stores or by mail order. Substrate should be replaced when necessary.

## Skin Shedding

Skin shedding is a normal part of skin behaviour, and it rarely causes problems. Shortly before the old skin is shed, it becomes dull and will develop a greyish sheen to it. The snake's eyes will also become an opaque blue because the eye scale – the brille, or tertiary spectacle – is also shed. This is because the new skin is growing beneath the old. The eyes will clear before the body skin is shed. When the new skin is ready, the snake will rub his face against something in the vivarium to break the skin, and will then crawl out of it.

It is important that no patches of old skin are left on the snake. Old skin can create a tourniquet effect, cutting off the blood supply and causing gangrene. Regular baths, or putting the snake in a wet pillowcase overnight, will soften the stubborn patch and encourage its removal. If in doubt, seek the advice of a veterinary surgeon.

Wild snakes rarely have difficulty shedding, but domestic snakes may experience problems if they are dehydrated, starving, in poor health, or if the vivarium humidity is too low.

## Going Away

Snakes need daily attention. If you are planning to go away, find a fellow snake enthusiast who will come in to check on your snake, clean the water bowl and remove faeces.

*A spray with an atomiser may help with skin-shedding.*

# Health Care

A healthy snake is described on page 20. The first signs of illness are lethargy or extended periods of food refusal. If your snake is showing these symptoms, or any other signs of illness, you should consult your veterinary surgeon without delay.

## Dietary Deficiencies

Because snakes consume their prey entirely, dietary deficiencies are fairly uncommon. However, mismanagement does lead to deficiencies. Twitching is a common sign, and the snake is also likely to throw itself on its back.

Discoloration or ulceration in the mouth are other symptoms. A poor diet can lead to many complications, resulting in death, so your snake should be seen by a vet without delay. If you are unsure whether you are feeding the correct diet, your vet or a snake expert should be consulted.

*Taiwan Beauty snake.*

*Red-sided Garter snake.*

## Intestinal Problems

When cleaning out the vivarium, it is worth checking any faecal deposits, as they can indicate ill-health in your snake. Look out for watery faeces or diarrhoea, which may have a strong odour and may be greenish in colour. Other signs may be loss of appetite, or vomiting. The culprit may be an amoeba which attacks the intestinal lining, and can kill your snake very quickly. Low temperatures and poor hygiene are usually responsible for reducing your snake's immunity. It is highly contagious, and you should consult your veterinary surgeon at once.

Internal parasites, such as worms, may also be responsible for intestinal problems. Your snake may eat but never put on weight, or may even lose weight, blood may be present in the faeces, as will tiny worms. Worm infestation is more common in wild-caught snakes. If you suspect worms, consult your veterinary surgeon, taking a faecal sample with you.

## Mouth Rot

Otherwise known as 'infectious necrotic stomatitis', mouth rot is potentially fatal. Caused by injury to the mouth, teeth or gums, bacteria then enters the wound and spreads to surrounding tissue. The area will become inflamed, dead skin inside the mouth will be shed, and pus will be emitted. Loss of appetite may result. Immediate veterinary advice should be sought.

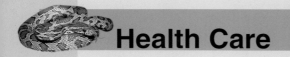
## Respiratory Problems

If your snake frequently has its mouth open, or is blowing bubbles from the mouth and nostrils, it may be suffering from a respiratory infection or lungworms. This sometimes happens if the snake is stressed, undernourished, weakened by egg-laying, or if the immune system has been affected by too low a temperature. If caught early enough, raising the temperature in the vivarium to around 88-89 degrees Fahrenheit/28-32 degrees Centigrade may resolve the problem.

Because most snakes only have one properly functioning lung, respiratory problems can be dangerous, and are a common cause of death in captive snakes. If symptoms persist, or worsen, immediate veterinary advice should be sought.

## Skin Problems

Pus under the scales, and the skin being discoloured or brown, are signs of scale rot. Blisters may also be seen. This is from an infection caused by a dirty or wet enclosure.

'Blister disease' is also caused by wet conditions. Blisters – sometimes quite large in size – on the underside of the snake can become infected and the condition can worsen.

In both conditions, prompt treatment by a vet is needed, as well as an immediate improvement in the snake's living conditions.

*Black Kingsnake.*

## Ticks And Mites

Snake mites are small, round, black parasites which are frequently seen on captive snakes. Specialist products are available to deal with them. As well as treating the snake, it is vital to disinfect the vivarium and decor to eliminate any eggs. The substrate should be replaced.

Ticks are less common. These are larger than mites and much easier to see. They bury their head in the host's skin, which makes them more difficult to remove. They can be taken out with tweezers, but care should be taken to ensure the head comes away properly, or infection could result. It is better to use a product to loosen them prior to attempting removal, such as Vaseline (pharmacy-grade petroleum jelly). If you are in any doubt, seek further veterinary help.

## Wounds

Wounds are commonly caused by
• An aggressive vivarium-mate
• Rubbing against the lid to escape
• Burns from an inappropriately placed basking lamp (or by using hot rocks – which should *never* be used in a vivarium with snakes).

If the wound is small, keep it clean and use an antibiotic ointment on it. Snake wounds generally heal quickly, and skin shedding aids the process. If it is a large injury, which may need stitches, or if it is infected, seek veterinary attention.